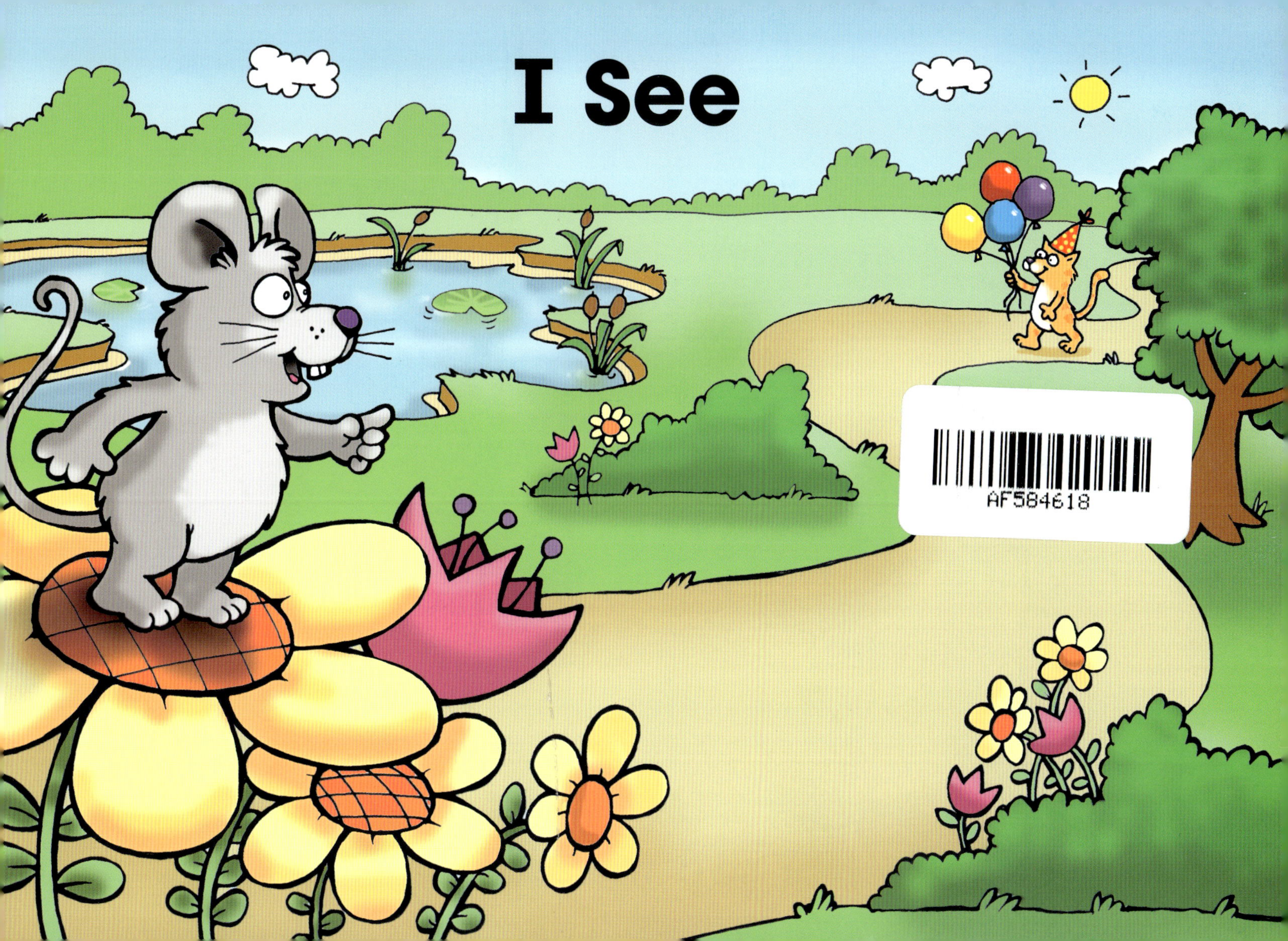
I See

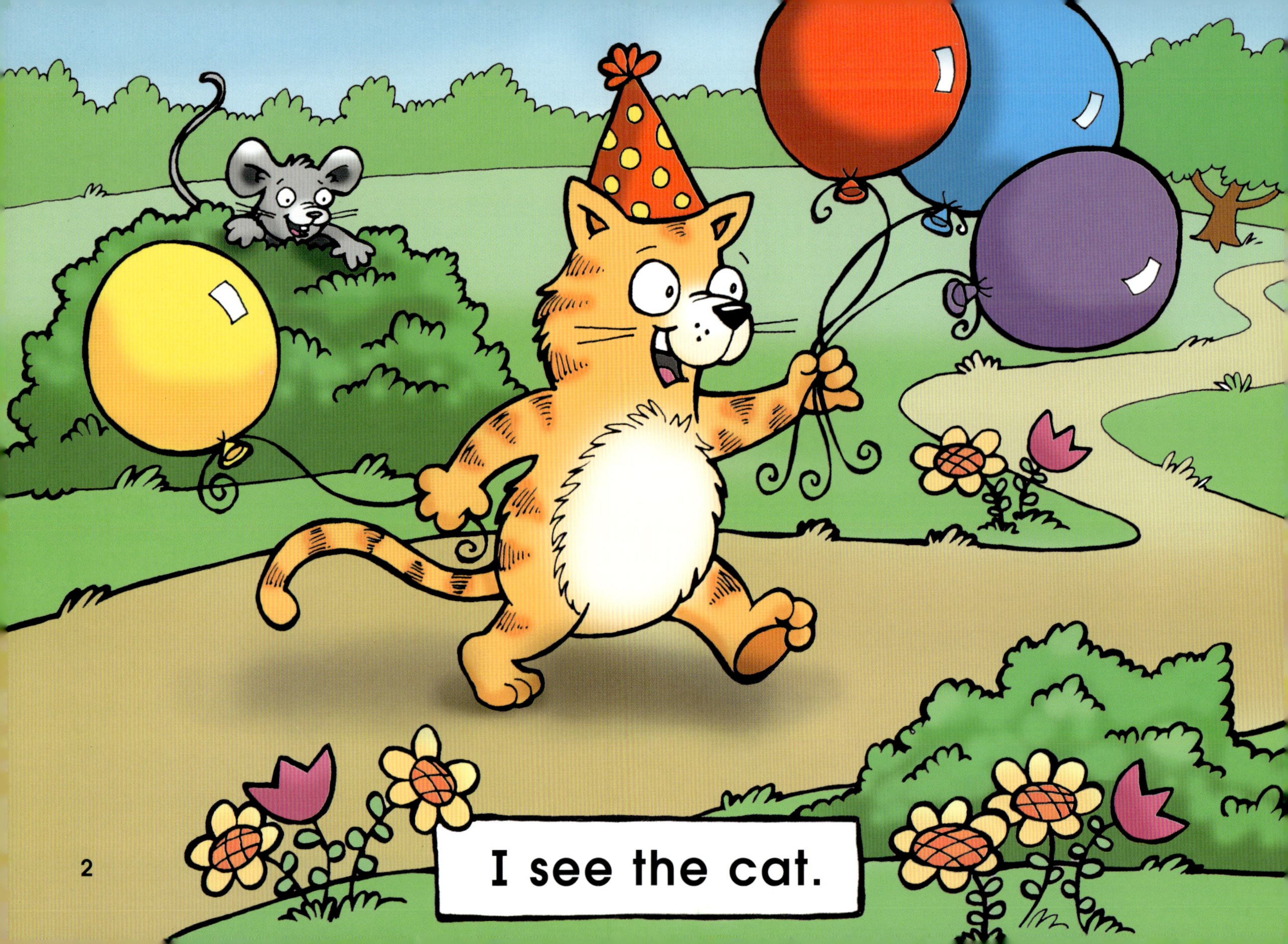

I see the cat.

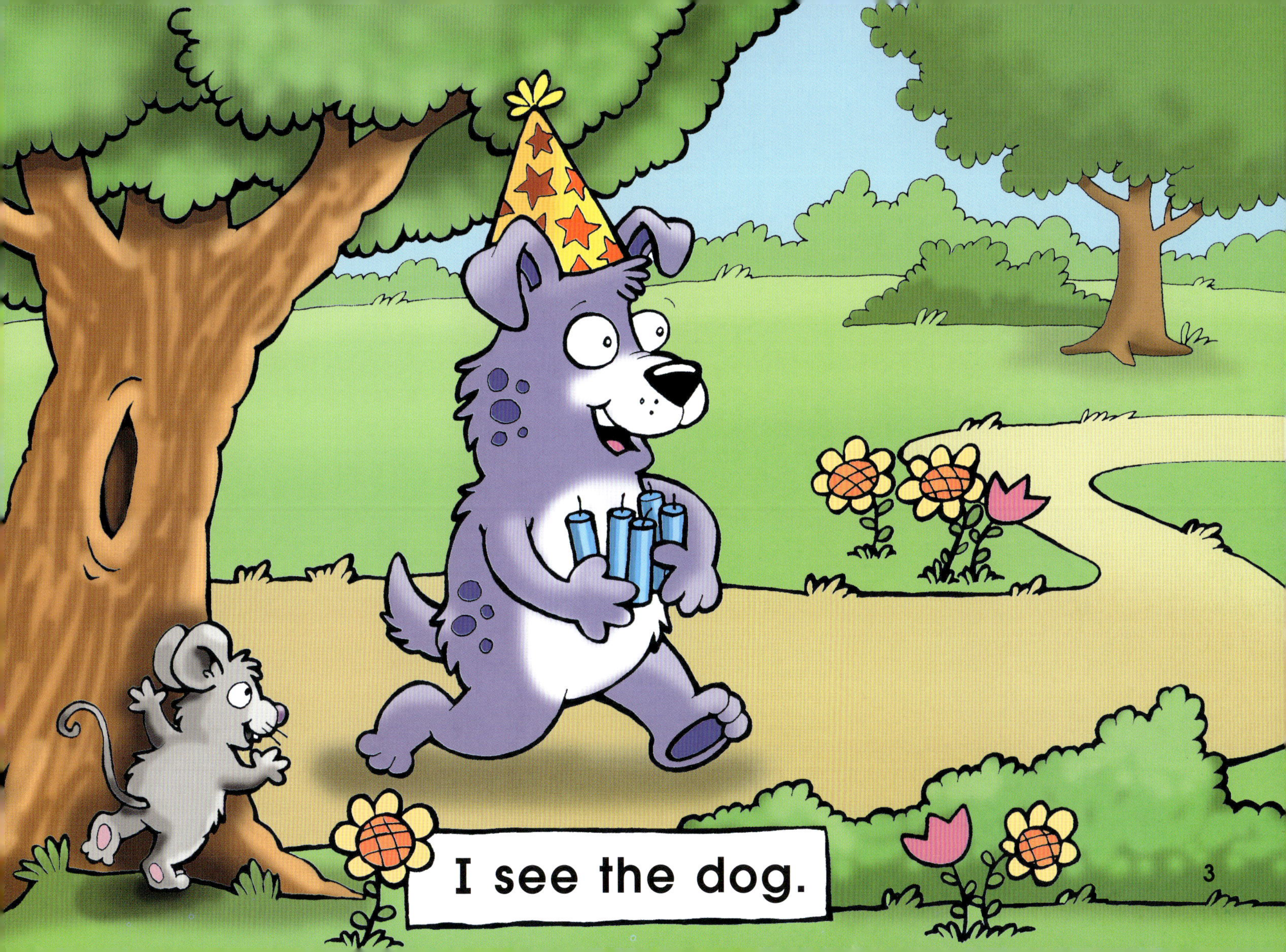

I see the dog.

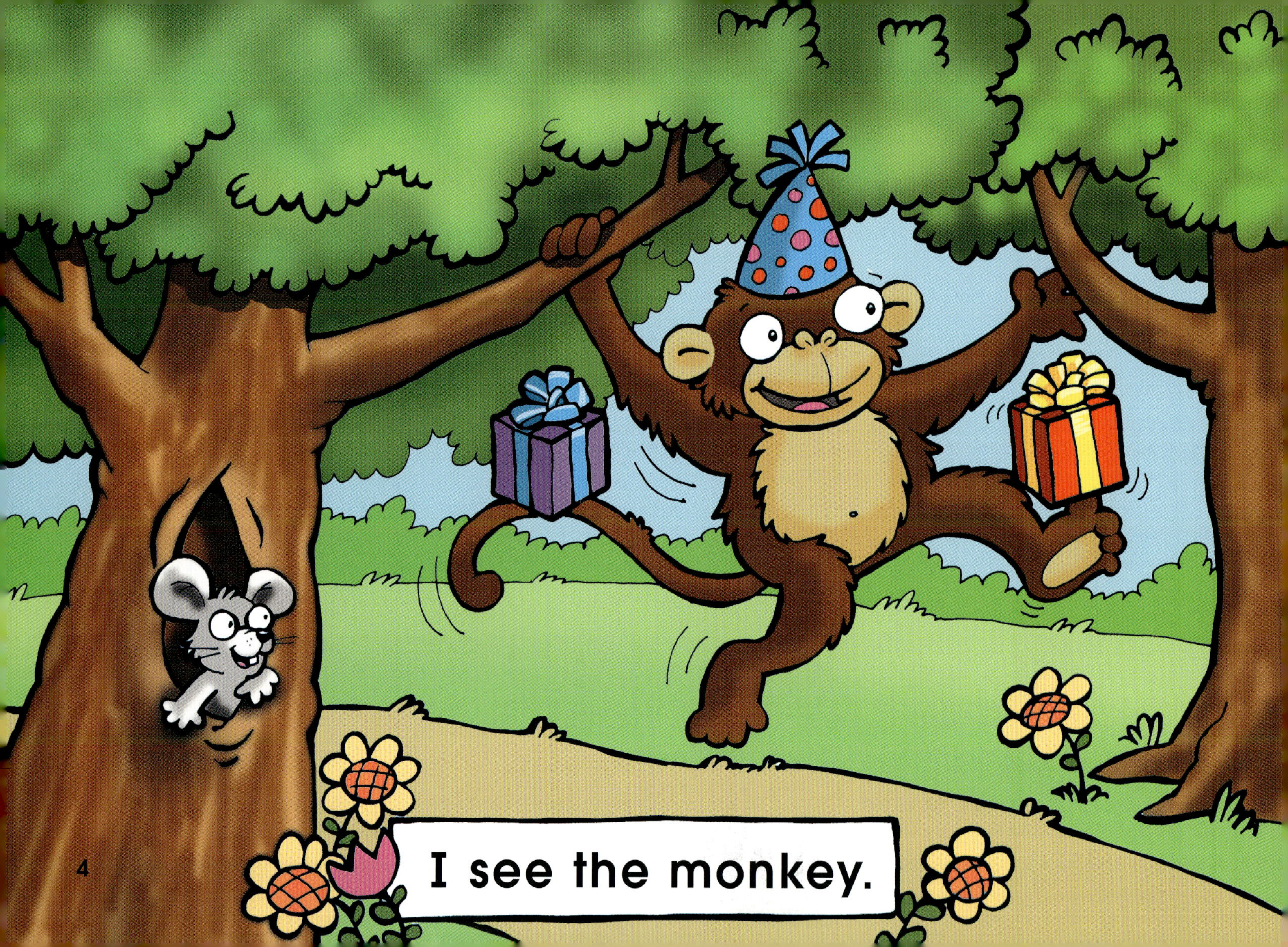
I see the monkey.

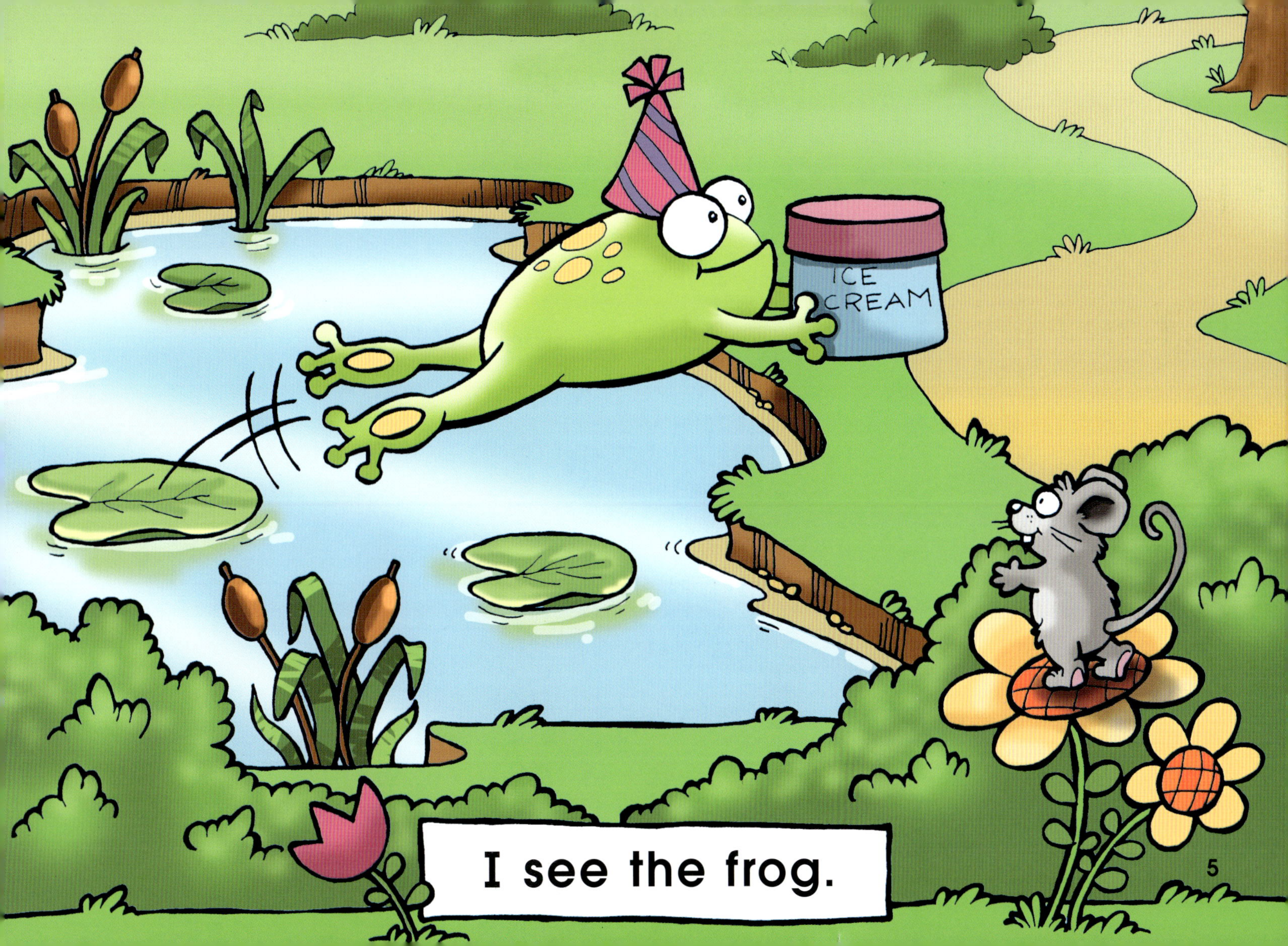

I see the frog.

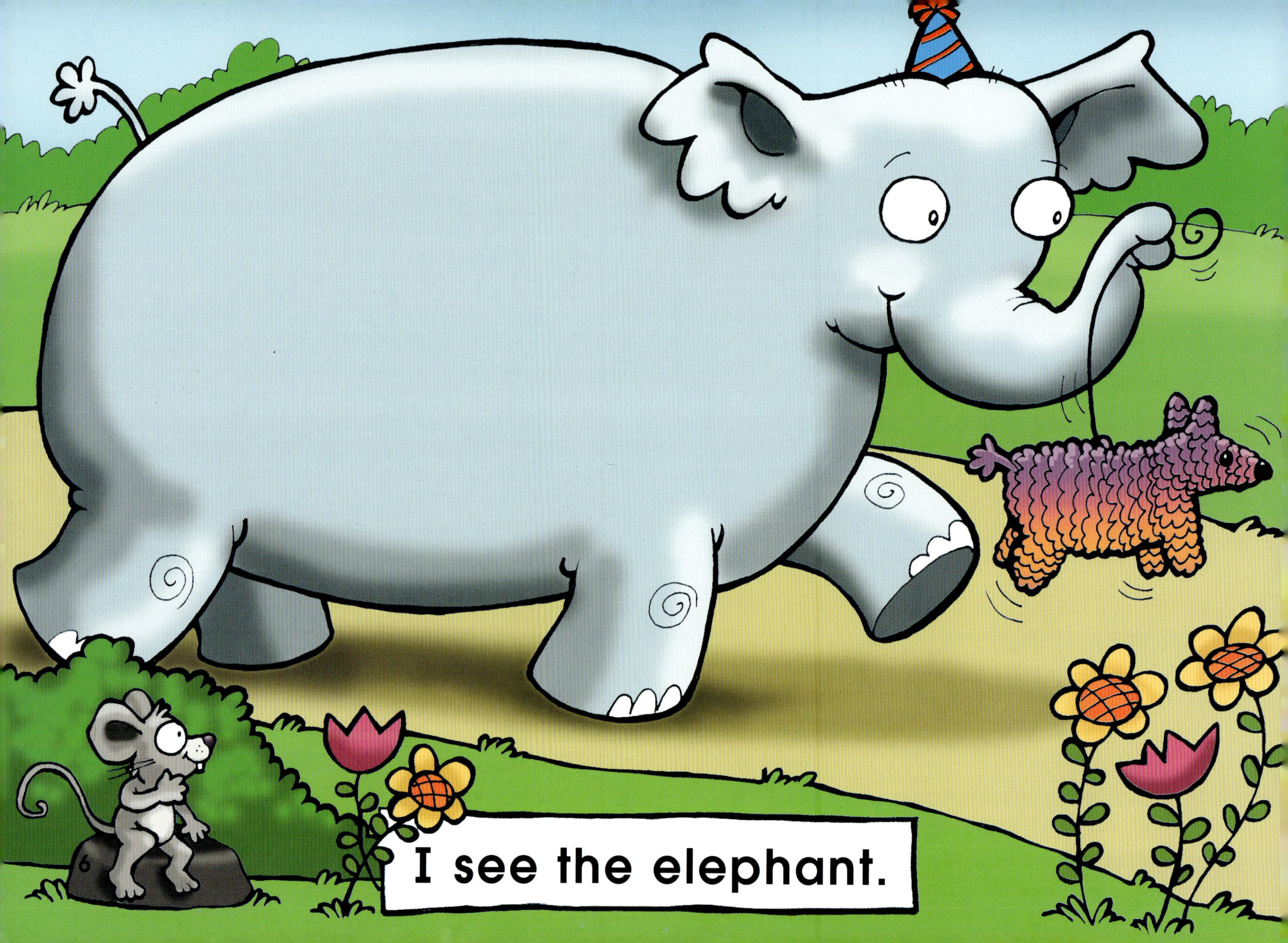
I see the elephant.

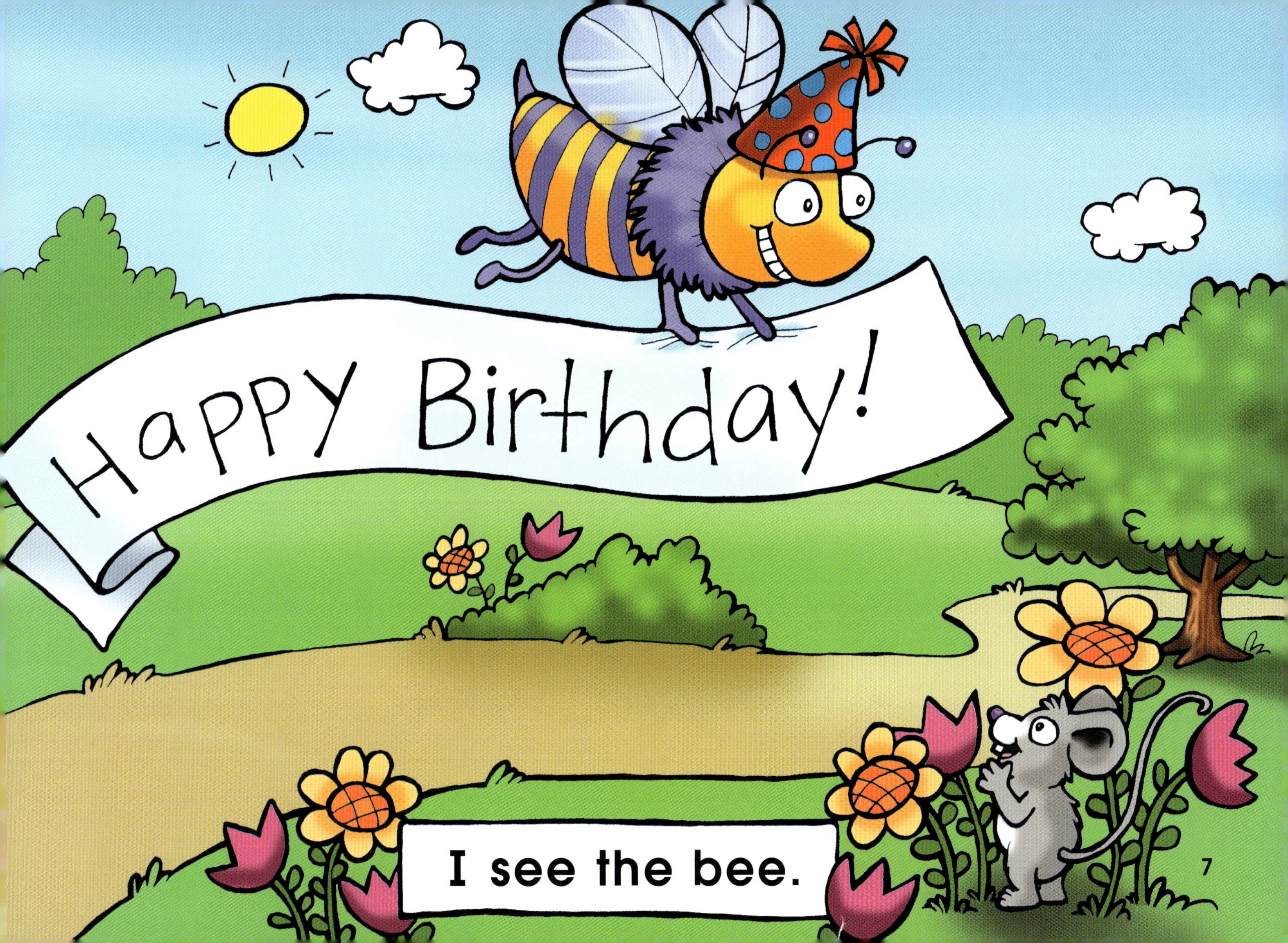

I see the bee.

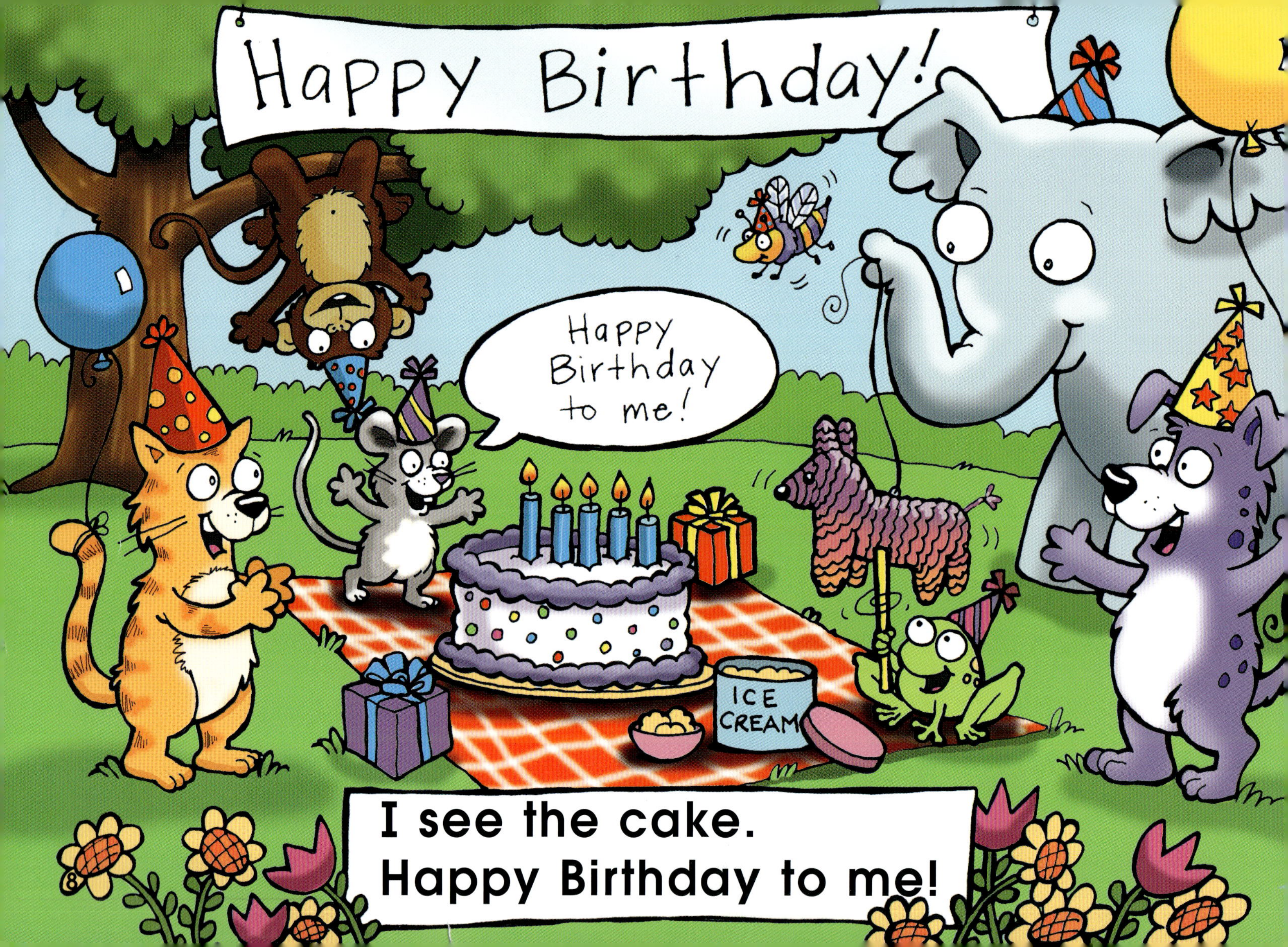

I see the cake.
Happy Birthday to me!